Deep Blue Heart

by

Diana Perry

Copyright © 2017 Diana Perry
All rights reserved.

ISBN-13: 978-1543240665
ISBN-10: 1543240666

DEDICATION

To anyone lost at sea,
and for those waiting onshore.
And for you,
I said I'd write about you someday.

CONTENTS

LIKE LIFE ITSELF	1
Looking back	3
Going	4
Wound	5
Detachment	6
In ruins	7
Monday morning blues	8
The story of us	9
I do	10
The uninvited	12
p.s.	13
Sickness	14
Palm reader	15
Waiting	16
Bird	17
Soldier	18
Unwanted	19
TracFone	20
I ache, too	21
OCD	22
Star	23
Brown-eyed nightmare	24
Before	26
Flinch	27
Man	28
Band-aid	29
The trouble with numbers	30
Between days	31

Crumbs	32
Outgrown	33
Glass	34
The usual	35
Starbuckssomething	36
Arrhythmia	37
Without	38
Disbelief	39
Thursday mornings at the library	40
Looking for salvation	41
Prayer	42
I was fine	43
Undone	44
Shaken, not stirred	45
Excerpt	46
Ugly	47
After you	48
Quiet things	49
With you	50
The end of the friendship	51
Maroon	52
With	53
Women	54
Flawless	56
Adam	57
Shadow	58
Easy	59
Keeper	60
Rob, or Missing in Miami	61
Waiting	62
Empty	63

Always, maybe	64
Someone	65
New Years Eve party	66
Note	67
Magnolia	68
Grave	69
Remind me	70
Migraine, for Ben	71
Enough	72
Girl between the lines	74
Ghost	75
What's left of what's left	76
Static	78
MORNING	79
Morning is a man	81
Redhead	82
The last day of the first marriage	83
Scar	84
Touch	85
Mornings, made silver	86
Searching	87
Rain	88
Across the miles	89
Out of everything	90
5 a.m.	91
Empty Space	92
Prayer	93
Hollow moons	94
Me without you	95

Jesus is waiting	96
Fog, rising	97
The way you sleep	98
Upstaged	99
Faith	100
Disbelief	101
Suspended	102
Bitterness	103
SEASICK	105
Of waves and war	107
For J's beach house	108
Almost	109
Oceans	110
All things beautiful	111
Key West, 2010	112
Bolt rope	113
Fury	114
Unsaid	115
Like water	116
Atlas	117
Harbor	118
North sea	120
St. somewhere	121
Seashell	122
Savior	123
Natural disaster	124
Beach town	125
Daniel's poem	126
St. Petersburg, FL	127

The old life	128
Deep blue something	129
Aftermath	130
Seasick	131
Doubt	132
S. Atlantic Ave.	133
After the storm	134
Sailor	135
Hurricane Matthew	136
July	138
Postcards	139
Forecast	140
Lighthouse	141
Promise	142
Dissonance	143
Westerly	144
Crinkle	145
Whitecaps	146
Message in a bottle	147
SEASONS	149
Leap year	151
Sideways	152
Fooled by February	153
East-coast Earthquakes	154
And love	155
Florida	156
June	157
Unmerry mermaid	158
Summertime blues	159

Locust poem	160
Some bar in St. Augustine	161
Owen, the Orca	162
Mid-Summer misery	163
Clearwater, FL	164
August moon	165
Parking lot	166
Deep sea divers, for Jimmy	168
Last year's poem	167
August 30th was a Thursday	168
Secrets	169
Silence in September	170
New Smyrna	171
Late-season low	172
Two autumns	173
Thief	174
Fallen	175
Dana California	176
Afterglow	177
Myself	178
Motorcycles in May	179
Stars of Hollywood	180
Flake	181
Homesick in Florida	182
Two months in Montauk	183
Someone up north	184
Wish list	185
Iceland	186
December in St. Pete	190
The last of the last	192
The way of everything	194

AFTER DARK 195

In orbit	197
Shhhh	198
Rush	200
Dirty poem	201
Mother Teresa	202
Midnight blue	204
Teeth	206
My gift to you	207
Can you feel me now?	208
Earthquake	209
Guilt	210
Madness	211
Fracture	212
Tightrope	213
Chevron incision	214
Moon	215
Liar	216
Gone	217
Suicide	218
Intruder	219
Not mine	220
Captain and Coke	221
Aching silence	222
Anyone	223
Forget this	224

LIKE LIFE ITSELF

*of course you can't,
and neither can i.*

-t.m. fisher

Diana Perry

Looking back

I am seventy-six and I've learned nothing
except how love is fleeting and that it
comes and goes in waves.

I go back in time and I am twenty-six again
and I now understand about this perfect weight
beneath my heart, I carried it inside
my very womb.

I have yet to learn
about the lonely hours between 4 and 6 a.m.
or the indifference of birds
and how to breathe through days
that feel like years.

I am seventy-six but I will always
be somewhere between twenty-five and now,
two yellow-haired angels smiling in one room,
a husband asleep in the next.
Vulnerable, like life itself.

The last day of autumn,
the first day of spring.
It will always be like this.

Going

I have grown older
and comfortable here,
these walls have rounded
to fit the shape
of my spine.

My palms know the
kitchen table
with its stains and nicks
and the clock on the wall—
how many years
did it tick?

I could have gone yesterday
or the day before,
but they've all grown
so dear to me:
the walls and the silence
and the clock out of time,
and the table—now down
on all fours.

Wound

This wound is opened up again,
sutures
undone
one by one.

Bitten flesh
and tendons, severed.

I breathe.
I wait. I wait. . .
Some things will hurt forever.

Detachment

Not often
but sometimes
I watch them.
They're beautiful
and lost
like me
and I think
Maybe
I'm not alone
Maybe
they're lost too
Sure and unsure
beautiful
with ugly underneath
and then they speak
and I'm alone
again.

In ruins

He kissed
my collarbones
and loved me
something fierce
and we spoke
of a future
and lied
through our teeth.

They say he hasn't smiled.
They say I don't ever sleep.

How impossible
to build towers
from ruins
once abandoned
due to
utter disrepair.

I feel him in my bones.
I miss him everywhere.

Monday morning blues
==

You wanted a poem
so I wrote you one.
You said you felt
the rest of your life
laid out before you,
saw it in your dreams
like the lovers you made up
in your heart.

You said your sad
was sadder than mine,
prettier and better
than mine
and I didn't argue that.

So I wrote you this poem
you never saw,
and one day
you were gone
like summer
   in September
like sugar
   in a coffee cup.

Gone,
like Sunday
on a Monday morning.

The story of us

Tell me something.
Write me maybe.
Write another poem,
perhaps one about me.

I will, ok, I will, I say
but then I never do.
These poems and stories
are starting to get to me.
It makes me a little crazy,
the way he begs for pieces
of me, in heart and on paper.

And I won't ever tell him this,
but I will save ours for last:
The story of us
is the best one yet,

because it is the worst.

I do

Watch me, but don't look.
Didn't I tell you?—don't wish for me,
I will hear you and appear.
Don't write me, ever
because I will be forced
and happy to tell you about
my daily train wrecks
and late night disasters
and I'll admit how good it feels
and how sick, how sick it is
to peel you off me,
to feel you strip yourself
from my insides again.

Leave me but leave me
the undying ache of knowing
that you only loved the idea
of having an idea of us.
And I promise I will never
(iwillalways) speak of you,
I will only (n)ever write of you.

And in the morning, find me.
You can visit wearing shoes
and your $500 suit
and I'll have you crying
on your knees, I'll have you
begging like some goddamned dog

because I'm the only one who says I do
to all your questions but one
and your heart will beat for me
and my heart will ache for no one.

The uninvited

You knew how to
entirely disappear
from my life
and then you show up
like a rash
and in old fashion
unexpected
and years later
I discover you
under my nails
and find you
in the side effects
of some pill
I don't take.
And when
the dizziness
subsides
and the ringing
in my ears
comes to an end
I write you
into a poem
where you hide
in the lines
and run off the page
and back
to your own life
again.

Deep Blue Heart

<u>p.s.</u>

I keep your letters
and your shirt.

The shirt
has lost its scent,
but the words
still smell like you.

Sickness

I have a fever
and I ache all over.

The last time
I felt this way
I was in love.

Palm reader

Trace
with your fingers
each line in my palm.

Over and over
until no matter
which future they hold
they will never
forget the touch
of your hands.

Waiting

In no time
—perhaps in a year or even two—
you will have forgotten
all of this.
You will not remember exactly
my tongue
my teeth
my touch
(this is what time will do).
The memories will become more vague
and easier to ignore,
and it won't always
hurt this much.

Bird

Drove all night and found me here,
all saltwater skin and crocodile tears.
Dove into me headfirst and handsome,
so helplessly handsome and sweet.
I sang you songs of home and heartbreak.
I've sat and watched you weep.

Rushed through your life,
brought me flowers and reasons to live.
Called me your bird, plucked
yellow feathers from my ribs.
Kiss me once more and don't tell.
Smile, then disappear.
Find me in the treetops
in another million years.

Soldier

His heart
was like an open wound.

Nothing
anyone wanted to touch,

but still
something that needed
tending to.

Unwanted

Today I went to the animal shelter
to say Hello and Goodbye to something
someone once called their friend.

There was a graying black mutt
named Felix, who—with aching hips—
now sleeps deaf and forgotten
on cold concrete floors and who will have
his life taken tomorrow, and not by his age.

Benny, the pig, who had to leave home
because he uprooted an entire backyard.

Toby, the pit bull, born blind and
with the sweetest soul you ever saw.

Max, whose tail draws circles
in his ecstatic lab-like fashion and
whose oblivion moves me to tears.

Monday will produce a brand-new list,
the unwanted replaced by more unwanted,
and my heart aches as I walk away,

leaving behind those who would never
have left those who left them here,
if only they had been given a choice.

TracFone

Today
you and I
fall through the cracks
in the sidewalk.

46 minutes
and zero days left
on the love that was ours
while counting down the hours.

Out of time from the start.
We were nothing.

I ache, too

How did you lose me,
he asks, and I say
Don't worry,
I still think of you as mine.
Don't worry,
I ache, too.

Time slides away, sometimes
and it isn't easy
to remember you.
To love you and not touch you.
To lose you and not forget you.

OCD

Count the stairs always
on your way up or
               d
                   o
                       w
                           n,
the years, the steps, the hours.
The cracks in the pavement,
the skipped heartbeats
and the second that falls
in between.

Count on the silence
that comes with disappearing,
the noise one makes
when—

            gone.

Star

Untouchable man.
Your fingers unlocked my heart.
You were nowhere near as good as me,
you were the tiny grain, turned star.
You will be nothing I will ever reach for now,
but I will keep you up in your sky, shining.

In the morning I want you
to be the first thing the sun touches
and the last one
the moon kisses goodbye.

Foolish man, my friend. . .
we were beautiful once, do you remember?
Some things collide, without touching.
Some things can never be.

Brown-eyed nightmare

Some women
don't
won't
can't—let me
be.

They only wish
they could hate
me, begging
for acceptance
with scissors drawn
behind their backs.

French-tipped morons.
Doe-eyed nightmares.
They stare me down,
their exterior
beautiful, a poster
a painting,
the inside
uncomfortable
and twitchy,
I can feel
the dissonance
from across a room.

I am a mother
a wife, a writer.

Aloof

and not fluent
in the language
of envy,
there's only so low
I will go.

Before

Let's say
we never met.

Let's pretend
we didn't know
what we knew
before we knew:
how your lips would feel
what your words would do.

You never loved me
You never left
And I'll forget.

Let's pretend we never met.

Flinch

I crave your gentle heart,
your tongue and thumbs
and shoulder blades.

I inhale. Exhale.
Wait...

And then— I don't want to,
but then— I love you again.

Here,
strangers read about you
and I swear I flinch
when I hear your name.

If it means anything—
I romanticize your loss.
I hold it dear.
And nothing at all has changed.

Man

You go on clear, I can wear you for days.
We haven't met yet and your attitude sucks
but I noticed
you smell nice and already my mind goes
places with you and I can feel
your whiskers against the insides
of my thighs.
I've died in your arms a thousand times.

I've died in your arms a thousand times.
Already, I know who you are.

Stay, but—don't love me.
Don't leave me—but go!
It was only one time it meant nothing
Do this harder, and longer, I love you
Quit fucking crying, I hate you
If you stay, I'll buy you 3 new pairs of shoes
But Baby. Baby—wait !

Already, I know who you are.
You haven't even said your name, but
it's always the same old blues with you.
Always the same, with you, and you.

Band-aid

I am okay now.
I'm over the worst of it

until the next worst of it.

The trouble with numbers

I try not to remember you.
I get in trouble when I do.
And I do.
Over and over again
I forget about you,
and on days like today
it's hard to think of it all.
I rearrange the weeks
and the numbers never add up.
I tried to prove you wrong,
but one and one makes two.

Between days

I have been unable to move
from one day to the next.
I remain between the hours
of your peacefulness and
those of my own utter disarray.

Oh, to be yours again.
To fall between your ribs
and into your heart again.

Keep me in that moment forever,
the silence so complete.
Let's pretend our hearts are soft,
held together by what once was.

Crumbs

Let's keep this love
a secret.
Let's forget
all about it
and pretend
it never happened.
And years from now
you can
smile that smile
that did me in
years ago
and I will let you
sweep me off my feet
and under the rug
once again.

Outgrown

We were constant
and easy,
like heartbeats
like midnight.
Smiles
spread thin
and silent.
Love,
two sizes
too small.

Glass

She sits
in a house of glass
writes
invisible poems
with fingerprints
on windowpanes
to a man
who will not read
about a love
that never was.

The usual

Face-first
I fell
in love
today,
heart
and
good intentions
flung to the wind
pre-hurricane.
Once
just once
undone
and done
and I have
nothing else
to say
except
perhaps
I fell in love
today.

Starbuckssomething

After
a week's worth of
headaches and isolation,
I rejoin the world.
I sit with them,
everyone's gone mad and filled
with dread and deadlines
and death and shit.
I can't be here.

I leave the table
and go home
to my own madness,
my own four walls,

my own two hands.
I am not like them.
I am not like them.
I've tried so hard
to like them
but
I only love myself.

Arrhythmia

Hearts like ours
are made to beat
for the sake of beating
in silence.

Imagine, mine
Touch, here.

The up and down
the in and out
like needle and thread
like need and threat.

Without

How much of me
will he miss?
There is
an entire life
we will never
get to have.

And the fact
that he will be
alive
somewhere
without me
seems somehow
catastrophic.

Disbelief

Don't think
I've not thought of you,
—the idea of us—
an eyelash wish.
I've traced the notion
of your hands
in mine
with my own
fingertips
and in another life
I have kissed your lips
no less than
never enough times.

I believe in your belief
that I am all you'll ever need,
but we are strangers.

Repeat after me:
We
are just strangers
bound together
by needless need
and disbelief.

Thursday mornings at the library

Six short years ago
with sleepless eyes and still
somehow shell-shocked
by motherhood,
I spent my Thursdays
here, between the sounds of
sing-alongs and lullabies.

4 years later I return weekly
and sometimes utterly lost,
to read and write. In silence.
(Really, to waste time.)
The small hand in mine
replaced by pens too dull
and Starbucks coffee gone cold.

Inside my four hours of freedom,
the songs now sing themselves
and the books on the shelves
stand covered in dust like
toy soldiers and the years inside
remain on their frayed pages,

and unlike me,
entirely unharmed by time.

<u>Looking for salvation</u>

Even as only a memory
my heart still aches
when you come back.

You were slow torture
on Tuesday mornings,
my love for you grown
twice its size by summer.
The taste of you
stayed on my tongue
for years to come.
You were not of this world,
but you—
you were and

You will always be
a Never. My Maybe.
A too-soon-something.
My sanctity.
Salvation.

Prayer

...
Know this:
When I wake up
and when I fall
asleep,
there is you.

And your name
is the story I tell
myself
over and over
again.

Whispered
like a promise.
Recited
like a prayer.

I was fine

I can't listen to your heart.
Hopeless and hopeful
you hold my hands gently
and before you drive me away
you show me how your fingers
align perfectly with mine
and I am fine,

I meant to tell you I was fine
before a touch so tender
turned me insane.

You graze my wrist
to see how warm,
you bite my lip
to see how soft.
You said you would not break us
but we are still so made of glass.

Undone

We were made
of knots and nots.

He pulled
the right strings
and watched me
u

   n-

      r a

          v

       e

          l.

Shaken, not stirred

In order to write
I need things
out of place,
off-kilter,
askew,
not right.
Silence
above the chaos
that screams
underneath.

The moon is half-full.
I am mostly empty.
All of it as usual,
everything in place.
I pour my world
into a cup,

>   I stir.
>   I write.
>   I shake.

Excerpt

Your unavailability
    enrages me.
        Infuriates.
      Intoxicates.

Ugly

This hopelessness stings
and my words betray.
I am the writer of lunatic tales.
Strip me down to nothing
again with filthy hands
that don't belong.

I know I've been ugly
and disfigured by love,
but tell me again that
I'm beautiful beneath it all.

Because it's not like I don't care.
It's not like I don't try.

After you

Losing you
was like watching
every single star
fall from the sky.

"I miss you sorely"
is all I will say,
but the truth is:

like a moonless night
or a bird
that drops, mid flight,
that's what my life
has been like.

Quiet things

Because
>you stomp your feet
>to make the world shake
>the white noise scares you
>but you like to watch
>the fires rage
>
>you sleepwalk through your days
>and forget the difference between
>the white keys and the black ones
>(this will make your soul ache)
>you find every excuse
>to no longer like anyone
>and you keep all the secrets
>that are best kept secret.

Because
>years ago you found yourself
>dead
> and decided to tell no one.

With you

Driving three extra miles
just to hear someone else's
song again.
A stranger said "tomorrow"
and I skipped orange sunsets
and the entire month of June.
Are you removed from your life
as much as you are mine?
   This rain fell for THIS tree
     This heart fell for THIS man
        (and one of them died).
I remember your teeth,
your tongue and thighs.
I have searched and found you
nowhere.
This is my salvation.
(In spirit I walk your life.)

The end of the friendship

A guy I know called me yesterday
and complained that I never answer
the phone anymore.
I said—I got a typewriter,
this is how I talk now.
He said he may get his own
and I said—Good luck. Goodbye. Call me.

This typewriter won't ring
and that's ok.
I never answer anyway.

Maroon

We were
two-sided hearts turned purple
and it's been
two years of silence
and two years of slow catastrophes
and I ask again

When does this cord get cut
and
Why does this heart not shut?

This is
what we should've had, but
you and I belonged
elsewhere.
I held your hands in shadows
and buried you bone-deep.
This is who we are still.
This is what I keep.

With

You
have been
with
for such a long time,

this
without
will
feel like death.

Diana Perry

<u>Women</u>

We are exes, witches, wives.
You watch us sit lonely
in car lines and waiting rooms,
in empty cafés and your kitchens.
We write letters and sign them
with Love, and your last name.
Your lives are busy and you
have no time for nonsense and
sometimes you wonder but won't ask
who we are, and our goodness angers you
and you want to know why
—why god why—
are we waiting so patiently, sitting
so perfectly like stone, like wilting flowers,
like forgotten umbrellas in June.

We carry your children and your laundry
up and down two flights of stairs.
We carry your burdens and you love us.
We carry your burdens and you hate us.
We tie your ties and hold your hands,
handle your childish rage and bills.
We are your sex, your sanctuary,
sacred things, filled to the brim
with sacrifice and sweetness.

Too much for you in our presence.
Too much of an absence when gone.

Deep Blue Heart

When asked about the most beautiful thing
you ever saw, you'll mention something small.
You'll say a car, maybe. A country.
You'll say something insignificant.
But your heart will fold and crinkle and you'll close
your eyes and think of oceans of hair,
you'll think of curves and kindness.

Flawless

We were beautiful,
although we didn't last
long enough.
Like all things perfect.

Adam

Adam is back with his dimples
and sweet words.
Just when I think I've lost him entirely,
he reappears and talks to me
as if 8 years hadn't passed
between the last goodbye
and this hello.

He once told me he'd make a good lover
and although he's never touched me,
he insists and I can see his smile
stretch across a hundred miles.
The return of Adam, and the thought of him
leaves me tripping up stairs and
falling down rabbit holes.

Adam—
I once stole your rib.
Adam—
I paid with my smile.
But here he is.
Finds me where he left me,
picks up where he left off
and leaves me stunned
and filled with girlish dreams
and hope.

Shadow

We both thought
I would forget you.
I didn't,
although I tried
mightily.
And here it is,
the memory of you.

Still lingering
on my skin.
Still seeping
into places
left open
and raw
by your anger
and love.

Easy

It's easy
to get them to love me.
All I need to be is insurmountable,
a poem they don't comprehend,
an ocean that can't be crossed.

All you need to know is
how to skin and strip yourself
of yourself,
how to be soft in the hard-to-reach places
and when to listen when they don't speak.

Keeper

I am the keeper
of tired hearts and
broken promises
and you tortured me
with your immense heartache
and beautiful sense
of absence.

I found for you
a delicate perfection
in want and with words
you needed and thought
would save you
(and couldn't).

Rob, or Missing in Miami

I know this writer,
a friend of mine,
he's alone in life
but nobody knows that,
and he lives down south
and his letters arrive
here, scattered
throughout the year.

When they stop, I call him.

He's not good, he says,
most times he tells me
he's dying of something.
Always one thing or another.

Fine, I say, you're fine.
The whole world dances
to your song
and you are lost,
you are just lost
between the spaces
of your words.

Waiting

You leave and I become
a little less.

I hold my breath.

But here is what I know
—what I always knew—

You will come back.
(You always do.)

Empty

These words are meaningless,
like an old lover's jaded touch:

By the time you allow them
to make you feel something,
they'll already matter
to somebody else.

Always, maybe

To this day
when they speak of you

my heart says
I love you

my lips say
I used to.

<u>Someone</u>

You were so handsome.
From below.
From above.

So easy to love.

You were so handsome,
that last night
in that life
that wasn't ours.

New Years Eve party

6 years later
and I'm still avoiding crowds.
Everyone is someone's

and you
are still
not mine.

Note

There is no end
to me and you.

Love does things
time can't undo.

Magnolia

Through all
that time has touched
and washed away:
you remain.

Still,
a faded whisper
on my lips.
On my hips
a tug
a pull
a forgotten memory
a sudden pain.

Like dry grass
in spring rain.

You are here.
Time goes by.
You remain.

<u>Grave</u>

One day
someone
will find our
shallow grave

and dig up

these bones
we tried
so hard
to bury
as secrets
and love
and lies.

Remind me

Remind me
of the nights we spent in silence
waiting for rain,
a revelation of the truth.
You and I,
getting to the bottom of it all.

Tell me
about how it used to be
before the darkness hit
before the world came to a halt,

when your words were yours
and not something
I made up in my mind
to fill the gaps of all
we never were and everything
we could have been.

Migraine, for Ben

You came
and went
and fell
like today
into tomorrow
and only you
had those eyes
and only you
looked at me
as if it was
the first time
and the last time
and now
I've got this ache
in my heart
and when they ask
I tell them
it's only
in my head.

Enough

We have
said
our goodbyes

but let me
  just say it
  again
  repeat the words
  one more time

let me cry
and fall
  to my knees
    fall
      to my death

let me
wipe my tears
with the bottom
of your pants
  and cling
  to your shoelaces

for love
for life
for love

let me caress

Deep Blue Heart

your heart
your hands

    just

    one

    last

    time.

Girl between the lines

I forgot you
because I had to.
We lived in letters, and died
with each and every written goodbye.
You, the man with the pen and I,
the nude girl who'd sit across
from you, cross-legged, red-haired
and overly rational, the way you liked me,
the way you said they should all be.
I, leaning languidly over your shoulder,
to get a better view of you.
There were holes in your story
and I found them and fell in and you
told me not to worry.

Now you get letters and they appear randomly
on sidewalks, and your cellphone
and they're not mine, they're not mailed by me.
I would never write you.
I would never remember to.
No words come to mind that should be yours.
You tell the world you loved me, in books.
I'm the girl pressed into every single page,
the one story you regret, the one you. . .

But—what does it matter to me, or you?
I forgot you.
Because I had to.

Ghost

It used to be
that I would find you
in all the soft spots of life
and in the seconds
between the cracks of
thunder and lightning
and silence.

I loved you, and I loved you
for all the wrong reasons.
Memories of memories folded,
and hidden in the cracks of time.

It's hell, I wrote you,
it's its own kind of hell
to choose the wrong thing
on purpose and with a smile
on my lips.

And it's Spring and then Winter
and Spring again and it's been years,
it's been years since then,
but your name remains heavy
like lead on the tip of my tongue.

And what you used to be to me
moves against me
in the dark.

What's left of what's left

Poor man on the corner,
walk over here when I pull up,
I'll turn my wallet upside down and
inside out for you.
Matter of fact, here, let me get out,
this car is yours now too.
Goodbye, you should consider heading east.

Cop in your cop car,
we see each other every morning,
and I've been so good you've
ignored me for months.
Today let me do something utterly strange
and incredibly stupid.
I'll make fun of you. I'll steal.
I'll undress in the back seat of your car.
I'll do anything, please, I'll take the ticket.
Give me one more, it's fun.

Here, black-haired girl with the Spanish accent,
yours—my blue eyes and red hair,
the typewriter, my clothes, my life,
the engagement rings and wedding bands,
try them on, don't you think they'd look gorgeous,
 worn on your own little left hand?

Take it all, it means nothing.
Really, I mean it, take everything

until there's not one thing left.

And soon you'll have forgotten
that it was ever mine at all.

Static

Cut the cord.
It's time.
Goodbye.

Ignore
... the heartbeats
... the static
... the sirens.

Goodbye
Goodbye!
You hear that,
Baby?
Thissssss—
 is radio silence.

MORNING

*it's how you wake in the morning,
making Cuban coffee and quiet.
stirring no milk, adding no sugar.
that's how you do. Buenos Dias.*

-t.m. fisher

Diana Perry

<u>Morning is a man</u>

Morning is a man,
it's come and gone
with its cold hands
and hot breath
moving like shadows
against my feverish skin.
Sort of numb, short lived
and already forgotten, once
before.

We were beautiful
in our imagined imperfections.
I like it best this way, he said,
when morning cracks us open
like an egg—fragile, thin
and unforgiving.
I love you, simply put and silent.

But isn't that easy to say
when mornings are fleeting
and nights belong
to someone else?

Redhead

The sun comes up
but its light
does not reach
you yet
there
on this side
of your bed,
does not fall yet
on bare skin
and someone
else's skin
you think of
and may not
touch again.
You are lost still
and nowhere
and you will wake
limbs tangled
to a mess
of blonde hair.
You'll love her
with eyes closed
in silence
and then you will
find me
everywhere.

The last day of the first marriage

The sun rose
like a half-smile;
its warmth
reaching me in places
someone I no longer know
will never touch me again.

Scar

He left a scratch
in my kitchen countertop,
forever reminding me
of the fact that he was
here once
and that now, he's not.
And every damn morning
I run my fingers over it
like a scar;
holding my coffee
in one hand,
and his memory
in the other.

Touch

Mornings are moments
and perpetual.
I feel everything
and everywhere
without ever
being touched
at all.

Mornings, made silver

Mornings down here are slow
and filled with sounds of sleep
and something more than silence.

At dawn, the moon dips into
the valley of your shoulder blades
and I watch it disappear and draw
silver ribbons across your chest.

When all else fails, when all else fades,
I will remember this: you and the moon
and mornings, made silver, and silence
that fell so effortlessly.

Searching

I've missed you
in one place
and then searched
for you
in others,
sifting through
stones and sand
and sadness,
not finding you
under rocks
and elsewhere
nowhere.

Day after day
floating in and out
of my nights and
into my mornings,
sleepwalking and
searching for you
in a million lonely
places.

Rain

Rain and regret
on a Wednesday morning
and you wake up
to your own beating heart
and the rhythm of it
sounds a little like lonely
and the weight of that
feels a lot like hell.

Across the miles

Morning leaves me vulnerable,
life can't be silent enough.
I hear the sun come up
and your heartbeat
—still—
from years ago
and miles away.
Rain falls
on all the things
that should have been.

Out of everything

I woke to rain
and with stars
in my eyes.

It's 4:16
and the storm
sits 300 miles
off the coast
of St. Pete.

Your memory
lies heavily
across
my chest.
This morning
has already
defeated me.

I'm running low
on coffee
and out of things
to say.

5 a.m.

I've taken up rising at 5 a.m.
where the dark hides the day's
imperfections,
and the words feel less like
blows.

Empty space

I fall asleep to the sound
of heartbeats that aren't yours
and the hand I feel in my hair
is only my own.
I awake and ache for you, always,
and I am painfully aware
of the spaces between my fingers
where yours should be.

You are not here, and that is
my first thought every morning.

Prayer

I wake
I smile
you slip away.

I lose track
of you
and time.

Plead into sheets.

"Please always be,
always please
be mine."

Hollow moons

In the morning
I hear the rain fall
and I force myself again
to memorize the smell of it,
the sounds,
the thunder,
as if to forget the beats
of someone's heart
I no longer know.

I turn languid
beneath heavy hands,
beneath hollow moons
and I know you know
because this isn't
the first time I've mistaken
somebody else's love
for yours.

<u>Me without you</u>

Half asleep,
I need
your hands
your lips
your touch.

I don't know
how much
of this me
without you
you without me
I can take.

This morning
hurts, it aches
eyes closed
dawn breaks.

The world
wakes,
trembles,
shakes.

Jesus is waiting

Sunday morning rain
and sweet talk
of angels and saints.
I'm a white-knuckled
shotgun bride
full of fury
full of grace.
I'm saving face.
I leave the sinners
and believers.

Somewhere,
Jesus waits.

Fog, rising

The nights have been filled with fog
rising, and the need for something else.
The hours are late, when the wind whips up
your name and the air smells of candles—fighting!—
fighting but dying I think,
in a hurricane.

The slow minutes of morning,
the endless hours of mourning for someone
not quite yet gone and the gray doves outside the
window in the rain make me laugh madly
and think of you again.
You are still here.

(You are still here.)

I have not yet mastered the art
of making you

—disappear!—

The way you sleep

It's not until morning,
but it's in the way it pushes
and curves into your spine,
and how you've ached like this
since yesterday or the day
you woke up and forgot
what it was you meant to keep.

It's in your empty hands
once your fingers uncurl,
you carry it in every desperate
and failed attempt of I will always
and in all the nevers you ever
spoke and left on lovers
you meant to love and didn't.

It's 4:59 and it's your very own hell
and it shows in the way you sleep.

Upstaged

Mornings were mine.
I used to rise and try
to beat the sun.

I would be the first
to kiss my sleeping
children's cheeks.
The first to run
my hands over every
brand new day.

I used to think
my love outshone
everything.

Faith

We had faith
in a different
kind of love.

I still pray
for you
on Sunday mornings.

You will find me
on my knees,
clutching cheap
hotel soap
to my chest.

Believing

in everything
we were,
in everything

we were not.

<u>Disbelief</u>

In the morning
I wake
tangled
in dreams
and disbelief.

Before the sun
can touch me

I wipe you
away

like sleep.

Suspended

It isn't until morning
when I find memories
of memories
in the creases
of where you've been.
Your teeth
and ribs
and heart
and hand
still are
and always will be
(to me)
the same.

But you move
like you do.
Leave here
unfinished
suspended
upended
and only I
and you
know every
-thing
we missed
and will
not feel
again.

Bitterness

In the mornings
we shared our coffee
and laughed about life
and I knew all his secrets
and he knew most of mine
and isn't it funny
how it could have
all been so easy,
cream and sugar
and bitter smiles?

SEASICK

*"The ocean calls,
I hear it in the hallways
and in my coffee cup.
It is relentless.
Soon I will hear nothing else."*

-Richard Marks

Diana Perry

Of waves and war

This is me before you
and without you,
getting on with life,
getting wrecked
on a Monday night
and clinging
to an anchor
the size of you.

My insides
are clinking
against the ice
in my drink
and these waves
of wanting you
are war.

<u>For J's beach house</u>

One day
(and it will be years from now)
you'll not be here
you'll be elsewhere
on a beach
on a Sunday
sand sifting
through your fingers
sun rays in your hair
and something
inside of you
will stir
will move you
monumental
like mountains
and you'll
recall me then
in a different light
from a different life
and how we used to say
that one day. . .
one day. . .
how somewhere else
we could've been
something else.

Almost

The rain took my wind chimes
and my lover's good faith
and the air presses against me

and holds the sticky sweetness
of white magnolias and the need
for something else.

The man who left me
pointed west before he went
and his last words to me were

Today is not a good day for swimming,
babe, we both saw
someone (this morning) nearly drowned.

He does not listen, I whisper
"But nearly, to me, means almost
and almost doesn't count."

Oceans

He came from
who knows where
into my life,
appeared like
a mercurial breeze,
lit my skies
in the darkest of nights.
Our paths perhaps meant
to cross
since the beginning of time,
drawn to each other
like moths to flame,
drawn into the lines
of my palm.
One look into his heart
and mine was his and I keep
us exactly there:
through time
and miles and country lines,
the distance between us
is fine, like hair.
His name means Ocean
and mine is the symbol of Rain
and I know of no world
in which one can exist
without the other.

All things beautiful

Tonight was blue on blue
and a sun that set and bled
violets and rubies into sand.

There is a hurricane 238 miles
offshore and the ocean lays large
and heavy across this idea of us,
its weight more unnerving than before,
now that we've become
so much greater of a thing.

Be the calm inside the storm, you said
and my days fill with whitecaps
and waves and thoughts of you,
damp-haired and delicious lips,
that taste like all things beautiful.

Key West, 2010

It was the year of
perpetual bliss. Solo cups
and paper plates in paradise

where the only thing
permanent were bad tattoos
and palm trees

and love was plastic and
disposable like empty bottles
of Panama Red.

<u>Bolt rope</u>

This morning
it's thunder
and writing
by candlelight
and I imagine this:
your heart is a compass
which I keep safe
inside my binnacle chest.
And there's a rope
and there are knots
and the rope
I imagine
is old,
and perhaps
it's existed
since the beginning
of time—
me, belayed
to you,
your heart
tethered
to mine.

Fury

The sky this morning was steel gray,
lonely and lovely, but still gray.
The Atlantic today
churned up with storms, full of fury
over entirely nothing.

I keep a glass filled with water nearby
and I think of oceans and imagine
you somewhere, in there, floating.

This morning I wrote you, angry,
and I imagined your face when
you read about the time I nearly broke
that glass and about the day
we never met.

Unsaid

Today
an ocean lies
between us
and a million things
left unsaid.

Like water

Perhaps
it was the waves
or the need
for something
more,
or the way
you spoke of stars
and how the ocean
leaked and soaked
our days
with distance
and desire.

You came to me,
scraped knees
and burning eyes
and I,
I took you in
and it wasn't
your fault
I let you win
or how you
filled my mind
with ease.
You.
A perfect fit,
like water.

Atlas

I feel your hands tremble,
still searching, still tracing
across maps, state lines,
oceans and continents.
Still asking yourself
where in the world I was
when you lost me.
Thinking, one day, you will find me.

If you were to look at a globe
I am where you would imagine
the heart to be.

Still
in all the places you left me.
Still
everywhere you failed to keep me.

Harbor

What I feel
for you now
comes
crashing
into me
like water,
moves me
like waves.
I am inland
still
and landlocked
and aching
for the sea.
I keep
my ocean eyes
fixed on
the horizon
and I tell myself
I see you
two thousand
miles east,
I imagine you
halfway home,
hull-down and
hopeful,
and it wasn't
until early
this morning,

that I could
think of you
and write you
this.

North Sea

The North Sea in June
was cold and unforgiving,
I was taught how to swim
in icy waters, among
brown algae and glaring eels.

Watch me, I am helpless.
See? I've grown numb with fear.

On Saturday nights
and over the years
I've lain in small bath tubs
all over the world and listened
to the sounds of my own
angry pulse, my beating heart,
underwater, amplified.

Watch me, I am helpless.
See? I've grown numb with fear.

<u>St. Somewhere</u>

Isn't it here where it began
on the shores of Sanibel Island?

St. Augustine, Sarasota,
St. Somewhere?

And doesn't it get old
doesn't it get cold

at night and sometimes
alone with nothing

but the same-same girl
and the same me-oh-my

and leftover love licked off
you like salt and lime?

I could have I should have
kissed you back then

but I can only do so much
and some wounds,

well, they just don't
heal.

Seashell

There was
the shell I found
in the shape of a heart
and a weight
I've memorized
that matched the shape
of you.

Everything
is broken now
but there are things
I long to tell you still.

Forgettable
and unimportant
and unlike anything
we were.

Savior

Sometimes
in order to be saved

you have to create
your own storms.

Natural disaster

This morning is
a race against time.
It's back to
nagging heartache
and natural disasters
with something
so monumental
just offshore,
looming
as a category 4
and threatening
the sanity of everyone.

Find me, I said, find me,
but the roar of the ocean
has grown too loud
and you are standing by,
silently watching,
and my words now fall
on distant shores,
too far
from where you are.

Beach town

Things are different here
by the ocean.
Times slows,
and people live in
coulds and
should-haves.
I watched a man
dr
o
 w
   n today.
I blew him a kiss
and he smiled madly,
one last time,
waving at the possibilities
and could have beens
of us.

Daniel's poem

In silence and suddenly
November crept in,
filled with northern lights
and new beginnings.
October left
a brand new mark on your skin
and you left a friend
and a ship and
an entire state behind
for 730 days of some
landlocked adventure
that lays four hours north
and leaves you un-reeving
and not looking back
and released at last
by stormy seas.
Tongue-tied and tired
you wave Norfolk
goodbye
and kiss the shore
just one last time.

St. Petersburg, FL

It isn't until I get to the water
that I can sit and think of this thing
how deep and where and why.
It's been so long,
what makes you hold on
what makes you still want to carry me
I ask and then you remember
that you must forget me entirely
and once again.

And then you call me two years later
and I don't answer because
I cannot talk about this one more time,
so I type this out and change the words
until they sound like something
I never meant to tell you.

You know I could never love you,
I say, but I did, I do!
and you, you lie and say
That's perfect
That's okay
'cause I could never love you, too.

The old life

One day you will read this
and your despair will stretch
from coast to coast
and ear to ear
and you'll remember
(won't you?)
the sounds of disaster
and the secrets we shared.

I now write in the rain for you
and black and white
are the colors I wear.
I, too, moved out of that old house.
I left our skeletons there.

<u>Deep blue something</u>

Why were we never together?
I could've woken up
every morning next to you,
every hurried early hour, spent
touching in darkness, tracing
the tattoos on your chest.

I never knew you, but
I loved you—
all sea-brine and beauty
all feather and down.
The bluest ocean between my
fingers, and your beating heart
below.

Aftermath

Every morning
and for one moment only
the room turns brilliant
and fills with your
brightness.
It used to be so easy
to watch you drape yourself
across the bed, dramatically,
wet hair and aftershave
and so far already from
what we once were.
One innocent kiss and I
could taste the storm in you
and knew—
of ruin and your own undoing
and how destruction would follow
and be inevitable.

<u>Seasick</u>

Something
is wrong now
I feel it
something
shook loose
and sloshing
back to front
with every step
to and fro
left and right
but not right.

And if I was a worrier
I'd be worried
but I don't worry
so much anymore.

This is fine
for now
I know
it's something
a little seasick
and splashy
there
not quite right
here,
inside.

Doubt

He said "Tomorrow"
and I skipped orange sunsets
and the entire month of June
only to meet once,
just once.
Forever
was two nights spent beneath
fireworks and summer skies,
where the beat of his heart
knew how to drown out
the sounds of the ocean and
those of any doubts.

He left me by the shore,
knowing we were both
happier there and told me
to look for him in the stars.
I didn't. I don't. I can't.
I close my eyes and say:
"I need you here.
I need you here.
I need you now."

S. Atlantic Ave.

This morning held promises,
I went running in the rain for you:
up and down A1A,
Sandpiper Lane
and back again.
A dog lay dying there,
matted fur, and terrified,
a half-gone, sad
little thing.
His brown dog eyes blinked
and I told him I was just
running, I said running away
and out of options, out on
you and away.
And then he died
(just like that: last breath,
gone. Last breath, done.)
and my heart skipped
and I laughed, madly
against the rain,
and all the way home.

After the storm

Friday felt like Sunday
and seemed like the end
of the world.
Through tears and sheets
of rain we sat and scanned
the sky for answers
and with cold fingers
circled the truth
over and over
like thumbs addicted
to the rim of a glass.
It could've been
so easy then, to fold,
to say the words, to throw
it all away, instead
we wasted candles and hours
on watching something
so substantial
twist and spin
out of control.

Sailor

I know you fell
overboard
(you did, you're here)
seasick and washed up
on my shore, salty,
and what you saw
when you looked
was wider
and deeper
than anything
you knew.
It shook you up
and pulled you under,
drowned you out,
and I will never tell you
that I loved you
always loved you
from the bottom
of my
deep
blue
heart.

Hurricane Matthew

The storm didn't come
but you did,
and everything was
sudden explosions and
oddly lovely and loud.

You should have
you could have
ruined me.
You know you sent cracks
running through my life.

Because I did
imagine, I do
still catch myself
thinking of you—
sitting on that bed,
beautiful and bare-
chested, breathing
and alive, writing,
always writing
about that ache you said
was written all over
my pretty fucking face.

You wrote those lines.
You put it there,
that ache.

And I did want you.
But only because
you could have
only because
you should have
ruined me,
entirely.

July

You and I
moved fast and slow,
twisted time
to match the beat of our hearts,
eyes closed to something
no one dared to see.
Go on, I said, you've
made your choice
but we breathed and lived
for all the wrong reasons
and you left for years
without looking back
and here you are now,
bittersweet perfection,
sullen and angry
like a Cat 3 hurricane
too far offshore
to be noticed,
sad and angry
like the hot tears
you once cried
so long ago
in July.

Postcards

I suppose
I should write something.
A poem, a letter.
A postcard.
Instead,
I lay on the beach,
get a drink, get buzzed,
get homesick,
get sad and sunburned
and write nothing
because I told you
I don't write anymore
because you told me
these poems, they
made me look crazy.
So I don't write anything
because I don't write
anymore.
Until I write this.

Forecast

Were we not
—all of us—
victims of weather
and want and
circumstance?

October 1st
and we can almost
breathe again
believe again
in low humidity
and hurricanes
and everyone's eyes
glued to TV screens
and forecast paths,
praying
the storm will spare us,
hoping
that it won't.

Lighthouse

Remember me,
waiting and unnoticed
on the edge of your horizon.
A ray of hope,
a glimpse of light.
A beacon.

Remember only
how from a distant shore
and in passing
I lit your face and
showed you diamonds
when what you knew
was darkness.

Remember me
as the calm inside
your very own storm.
Think of me
as a time of
hope.

Promise
=======

You'll
see me again,
your heart
is my harbor,
you said.

Without you
the days
are beginning
to stretch
like a sheet
across
an empty bed.

I miss you
terribly
(in the morning
in the madness
in allthespacesicannotfill).

Dissonance

This is just
another Sunday morning
in September.
You long for something
and leave me lost
and writing letters
from the shores
of Saint Augustine.
(Another bottle
with a poem flung
into the waves.)

The dissonance
in this silence
is dangerous
and disconcerting,
and the sunrise
this morning
simply
too lonely
and a little bit
too loud.

Westerly

There's a slow drizzle
outside my window.
It will not dissipate.
It cannot kill distance.
Or time.

I have a heart that stretches
for miles and reaches for
something across the sea.
I measure its beats in knots.
The rush of blood, like squalls.

This, this whatever this is
—thiswantthislovethislovethisneed—
came with the westerly gales
and stays
anchored down
inside of me.

Undoes me
and bends the year
into the shape

of something so great
it cannot be contained.

Crinkle

I never breathed you
in (or out)
and we are strangers
still, reacquainted
by time and tales
and you stole
my smile
and I took yours
and laid it down
side by side,
yours with yours,
mine with mine.

And if oceans
were seamless
and distance
didn't mean
what it meant
the world would
only for a flash
bend
only for a blink
inhale
exhale
gasp and crink-
le.

Whitecaps

It's been—
you've had a terrible year
and it shows in the way
you sleep at night.
The pull of the moon
takes you away again
and you sink into
a deepbluesomething
and swim among the stars.
Low tide (and lonely)
comes and goes
and some part of you
has curled up inside.

And now I write to you
from this shore.
You're elsewhere
and I think of two ships
passing in the dark.
I think of whitecaps
and capsized things
to say and there's a reef
and teeth and undertow.

And if I see your flares
in a midnight sky—
I'll come. I'll keep you safe,
down inside my ocean eyes.

Message in a bottle

Your love for me
was like a secret message
in a bottle,
thrown into the ocean.

Forever lost,
unchartable
and undiscovered.

Sinking
somewhere
to the bottom of the sea.

It had meant nothing.

SEASONS

*it's still something. it's still nothing.
i found you;
too late.*

-Matthew Owen Smith

Leap year

We had a leap year
kind of love.
Extraordinary.
Insignificant.
The type you only
remember
when something else
reminds you.

I am here
to remind you.

I am
all the lines
in all the songs
you never knew.

Sideways

The world touches me
and I touch nothing
in return.

I lost my phone
with 500 poems
and a dream in a dream
and a made-up friend.

I broke my knuckle
and a promise
and the green vase
from St. Augustine
and a heart that lay
sideways in its chest.

I lost my phone.
I broke such and such bone
I broke a vase and a promise:

I said
"Winter always hurts
the worst, but
you'll be healed
by Summer."

Fooled by February

My heart's gone cold.
Its branches,
splintered.

Perpetual winter.

There is nothing
here to find,
nothing worth knowing.

March
in like Spring.
And keep going.

East-coast Earthquakes

This means nothing.
We took (from their lives)
three days and somehow
saved ourselves
and stayed the furthest away
from anywhere else.

Blind to the truth
and thumbs run over
old wounds
left by the slow tear
of time
and it's come
down to old promises
and broken bones.

This still means nothing
to anyone
but I will tell you now
that you are safe,
that nothing was lost
and that there will be
no scars.

Listen. Today
the world did not shake.
Nobody's but ours.

<u>And love</u>

Stay.
Don't go.
I need you
to keep telling me
things.

Words
of things
that last forever

unlike Sundays
and Summers
and love.

Florida

When you're from somewhere else,
Sundays have a different feel.
You grow sick of Summer by June
and the way August sticks to you
with its persistence and new sense
of nuisance.

You see seagulls lost in parking lots
50 miles east of the ocean,
misplaced or not, you'll wonder
for the rest of your life.

And if you're good at math and numbers
you'll understand the drop
in barometric pressure,
the departure from normal and the
number of named storms that never come,
that drown out in the Atlantic
or disappear into the Gulf.

And if you're good with numbers
you'll find out soon enough
that it only takes one hand to know
that one and one makes two
and that none of it makes sense.

June

We are six months in
and this relentless heat
rises off the ground
and attaches to our skin.

You frown at the way the sun
gets caught in my hair
and I'm high on last year's
heartache and this mornings
antihistamines

and I remember 12 months
of misery or perhaps
twenty-four of this unease

and I'm writing today
to remind you of how June
breaks our bones
—annually—

and brings us to our knees.

Unmerry Mermaid

Black algae
and I'm
an unmerry
mermaid
scraping knuckles
bloody
on rough turquoise walls.
A myriad of
dark spots
spread
and every dot
beneath my
fingertips
turns into
a reminder
of my downfalls
and failures.
Red-haired fury
echoing
against barriers
of baby-blues.
Above the surface
the palm trees
sway, lazily.

Below,
the siren
screams.

Summertime Blues

We fell
    in love
as fast as we
       fell apart.

I broke to pieces
alongside him
in the summertime
and I would crack

my own bones today
to make them
somehow fit
into his again.

Locust poem

The lady next door
has an old dog and blue hair.
She sees me out in the yard
and people think
just because you're out there
alive, breathing, you want to
talk.
She asks if I've been hearing
those damn locusts at night,
she says she gets no sleep.
I say, Yes—yes I hear them,
of course I hear them,
daytime too. Yes,
the buzzing is
unbearable, Charlotte—and
so is everything else.

Some bar in St. Augustine

I remember
when time moved
counterclockwise
and the drunk blonde
to the left of you
who argued with the man
to my right;

the way you held my hand
under that table
and how, after, we went
back to being strangers
who knew everything
but how to connect
the dots.

Owen, the Orca

For three years
he had been mine.
Unhappy and only
half-alive,
I kept him
in the pool out back.

On Summer evenings
I watched him,
some mornings
I swam beside him.

He was never
within my reach
but he was always
much too close,

unhealthily
held captive,
my inhumanely
detained.

Today they found me
floating.
(To think I almost
loved him once.)

Mid-Summer misery

Summer has lulled our spirits
and dampened our sheets,
left dandelion seeds in our hair.

We, here, hold cold hearts
in our hands and lift them
to the sky,
wishing on stars that fall too fast
and land in places behind clouds.

I saw the sun rise above your chest
and watched it disappear again
somewhere between the horizon
and your shoulder blades.

You don't belong here.
You smell of smoke and fire
and you leave,
and I,
am left here,
ocean and horizon, with your heart
sewn to my sleeve.

Clearwater, FL

Scorching heat
and the slow torture
of your hands.

The ocean's blue
and I'm in love

and Summer's never
hurt this much.

August moon

It began
with the last breath
of last year's
last love
and ends today.

Between
two mason jars
and the moon

.

.

.

I bury you.

Parking lot

August again
Summertime
lost in this love
and humidity and rain
and you remain
in my thoughts
and your name
is etched into
everything.
Put back together
and saved
by your hands
again
in a backseat
years ago,
stretched between
right and wrong
with everything
at stake.
This despair knows
how to linger
and curls around me
like a snake
and your words bruise
and sting
when you talk about
how things
should have been.

I shiver
and I just can't shake you.
The years go by
and I still can't shake you.

Deep sea divers, for Jimmy

We sink and lie
like catfish
at the bottom
of some pool
out back
and we are
12 ft under
and we wait
and watch
the storms
roll in, roll over
and out again.

June, July,
August into Fall,
summer wasted,
waterlogged,
submerged
in this state
of constant
discontent
but we've learnt
and grown
quite good at this:

Life taught us early
to sink, to swim,
to hold our breath.

<u>Last year's poem</u>

These humid days
linger around like a stray dog,
and this entire summer
has been agony
with long days
and even longer nights,
but I can't shake the feeling
of something better up ahead,
because here we are,
August,
and he says
"Come find me in September!"
and I may
I might
I will.

August 30th was a Thursday

Darling Boy,
Sweet sunflower child.
Born before the world
turned to ashes
before
my very own eyes
and my hope
started to drop
like leaves.
You traded in your fins
in time and made it here
just before Summer
ran out on August
and I—
out of reasons to live.

Secrets

This morning
was goosebumps
and Autumn's first chill

and we kept undercover
our hands
and cold hearts.

Silence in September

You leave with Summer
but not without ease
and this sudden absence
of you and the shift
in sunlight stuns me

lulls me to sleep in shadows
brings with it falling leaves
brings me to my knees,
this September breeze
takes our old tears

and brings with it new things
we've not seen in years.
This silence unravels my senses,
leaves me sick for something,
defenseless.

New Smyrna

Bruised by Summer's end
and Sunday,
with sand in my teeth
and salt on my tongue,
I stand by the ocean
and watch the waves
swallow up
the ghosts of lovers
and unread letters
and the last
of last year's love.

Late-season low

Mid-September,
but Summer
is still all over me,
with Atlantic lows
and afternoon rains
and the way this humidity
leaves me irritated
and this waiting
for something
stains my days.

My heart is heavy now,
anchored down, grown
seasick, and stubborn
but I know
I know
you'll return with Fall
you'll come back
with everything
I've missed.
My sailor, my heart,
I ache
to lick the sea
off your skin.

Two autumns

Summer and palm trees could not stop
the tears, could not heal the pain.
Caution and cold promises tossed
into the sea and one would think
that it would have been easier
to rid myself of this,
should have been easier
to peel you off my skin.

We were so wrong and lost in the rip tide
and to watch us drown out there and sink
should have been the end of us,
should have been the only thing.

But 2 years slipped by and life wedged
itself between then and this
and 2 Autumns fell and brought you back
to everywhere I am, again
and all the things we should have been
and everything you've missed.

Thief

Summer
has left us
feeling in-
sanguine
and sick
and yet—
each year
we dread
Autumn
with its every
fallen
pretty
leaf.

Fall,
the way
it steals away
the beauty
of August
and then
leaves us,
creeping away
like a thief.

Fallen

I fall
and then
    I fall
again.

Like a snowflake
in the summertime.

I don't linger
I don't last
Like love
I'm already gone.

Dana California

It's October
and I can feel
myself
fall again
the way
September did,
and I catch
my breath
and think of
last year's heartache
and LA earthquakes
an East Coast rain.
Separated by so much more
than three hours and miles,
but bound together,
 nevertheless.
My sun is yours, you said
and I miss you
(I miss you terribly)
and I keep my eyes
on the sky
and believe again
in mild New York winters
and California Sundays,
in love and everything
we were back then.

Afterglow

The streets are empty.
The city is mine again.

Your name remains
gone, however

still etched
into
everything.

The dull ache,
the hollow sound,
pure white
afterglow.

I feel it all.
I feel it all.

On my way out.
On my way down.

Myself

It is October
and you are gone

and I fall entirely

into myself
again.

Motorcycles in May

The wind chimes outside
have begun to sound too much
like church bells in spring.

On this Sunday morning
I think of you, six hours ahead
and an ocean away.

The truth is that you lie
buried in snow and covered
in something more than despair.

Your vengeance came easy
today, the thought of you and
dandelions, the smell of fury
and gasoline.

Stars of Hollywood

You told me once. I know.
I remember. Years ago.
You said everything hurts and nothing helps.
So you go, and do this to make up for it:

You drive home with your eyes closed.
In December you make it into the city barefooted and
alarmingly brazen.
They find you in a ditch, naked and weeping, sleeping,
right there on the side of the road.

Or you wake up face down,
drunk in a stranger's bed, and bruised
and you can't remember your name
but you ache all over and that makes
you smile and the years pass, like this,
like those cars in the dark,
by that field you don't recall
and you don't believe in love
and you don't believe in looking back.

Sometimes you call to say sometimes
it helps to forget your pills,
and sometimes to swallow all of them
at once.

(You thought the stars were your friends.)

Flake

Winter came
and we woke
to frozen flowers
on window panes.

Who knew
that for days
we would not
leave the house

and how for years
you would not
leave me.

Homesick in Florida

This December is like most others
down here, still warm
and wrapped in red hibiscus.

The egrets have made a home
in our yards and the robins
appear, then vanish.

It's finding seashells on Sundays
and the lack of lightning storms
and rain.
It's oranges and sunshine and
Christmas carols in a summer dress.

It's feeling homesick and happy
and an occasional postcard from
elsewhere.
It's poinsettias and disappointment,
and it's all just more of the same.

Two months in Montauk

I liked you mostly
in the mornings
when you were
someone else
and elsewhere.
Half-asleep
and only mostly
in love
we were doomed
in the most
delicious ways.
The mere mention
of your name
undoes me still
unravels years
of raging demand.
The worst has happened
and the worst
has happened
and it wasn't even
that bad.

Someone up north

There is nothing like mourning
in Michigan.
The chill in the air leaves you
baffled and breathless,
it's half-expected but shakes
your bones.
Every winter and each day,
you wake up, surprised again
to find layers of ice
on your window panes
and yourself under inches
of snow.

The cold hurts and nothing
helps, you hang your head
against the freezing drizzle
of December and despair,
and you walk through your life
with frozen ground crunching
beneath the weight of your boots.

This is almost over.
This is almost done.

In a song and a pair of brown eyes,
in the barren trees out back:

Hope is hung.

Wish list

A game named
Patience
pajamas
binoculars
a bottle of Baileys
and library card.

Mittens, marbles
lap dance how-to
lava lamp and
licorice.

Lotto tickets
lexicon
a cactus
calendar
chemistry kit.

Iceland

You're gone
and I don't know
where to,
but there's a letter
and a postcard
with a picture
of a man
who waves
out a window
of a blue house
by the coast,
and how many times
I've imagined
this man
to be you
I can't tell

but I wave back
and say
Don't think
I'll forget you,
don't worry,
I won't.
And then
I fall asleep
and the man
on paper
turns out

my lights
and he stays up
and smiles
because he—
he came
from somewhere
else
and knows
everything
I don't.

December in St. Pete

You won't, but I do,
remember that night
you saved me.
You drove us west,
no further, but still
as far west as we could go
and it was December and we
were alone, the ocean and us,
and you laid me down
along the shore and tried
your hardest to explain.

Your face was lit by moonlight
and my skin was cold and
white as snow.
You'd stare and say—You're beautiful,
god, you're beautiful—
me, the girl who'd always beg you
to let her go.
(Don't leave yet, stay, go Go!)

And it was glorious, still is,
when I think of it now, the way
you fucked me against the
loneliness that laid buried
beneath me,
and I remember you now,
coming, and

going. Here,
but not.
Rising and falling
above me.

Years later, and I still shiver.
Still, you fall off me
like sand.

The last of the last

Has it not grown so heavy inside of you,
by the end of December, so plump and unbearably fat?
Did it not leave you fed up and frightened
and so filled with disgust,
don't you just want to yank it out now
like an unwanted infant, like an
intruder who took over your house?

What did you learn this year, besides how lucky you
are, and what do you know now that none of us knew
the year before,
really, tell me—what's changed?
Don't you still wake every morning, in shock,
unchanged and unfazed,
like a bad actor feigning surprise?

I invite you to come over tonight.
I know you've followed me home.
I've kept the doors locked and sometimes
open to you, I'll teach you to love with eyes closed.

Don't you wish you knew the underneath
of me, don't you wish sometimes
you could leave your house in the morning without
wanting to weep
at the thought of having to face the world?

Happy new year, let's you and me
drink to damage and love.
3
2
1
Cheers, my friend. I'll show you.
Come watch my stomach drop.

The way of everything

Words are heard
and turn deaf.

Things come and go
like tides and moons.

Here, then gone
like ebb and flow.

Eyes open. Close.

Someone lived here
once and left.

AFTER DARK

"I've forgotten nothing of you."

-t.m. fisher

Diana Perry

In orbit

In dreams you spring up like ivy,
roots twisting down below into
the great unknown.
Who knew the depth of you?
From distant shores you tug on me
and push me into the first week of winter.
Your name, a splinter in my hand.
A petal crushed and put away
until April, and May. Or June.

You were the stained glass window
in an empty church,
the one who caught
only the light of the moon.
You could have been the moons'
but I believe mostly you were mine.
I pray to you at night, and you don't
ever listen and I still don't understand.

There are some things I'll always know.
You were some kind of wonder.
On my horizon, but out of view.
Impossible and iridescent, invisible
to the naked eye.
I, a little dramatic. Well, very.
But you — a satellite.
The one who never
returned.

Shhhh

My idea of you
so violently
so desperately
loved your idea
of me.

I wished for you
so long ago,
I heard you calling me
from every corner
of this house.

Again,
you show up
in my dreams,
on the left side
of the bed.
Propped up
on an elbow,
watching me,
seeing me.

You see me.
Listen.
You know.

What?

You already know.
You always knew.

Listen.
Shhhh.
You don't hear it now.
But you will.
(You're mine.)

I wear you inside out.

Rush

It's rotten
but it's become
a rushed and
red-cheeked
morning routine.

"I don't love you.
And I don't read you."

My frayed letters
sniffed and read,
kicked and stashed
under your bed.

Pretentious
and pretty,
like black satin
thongs.

Dirty poem

10pm
it's raining here
and I think of you
again
out of sight
out of reach
and elsewhere.

I'm impatient
and wrapped
in heat
and it is now
that I want
these pink clouds
to open up
the sky to cum

down on you
and spread
across you
hot and wet
and wanting,
heaven
uncrossed and

open,
like a pair
of legs.

Mother Teresa

It burns holes
in your pockets
doesn't it?

It won't leave
your tongue,
your mouth
and lips, it doesn't
ever leave
you, does it ?

The way her name
is shaped like
lightning
and how it chars
you in all the right
places.

Can't you
feel it now
the scorch
inside your hand
and down your throat
into your soul

and don't you wish
now for a girl like me

who, with her lips,
could draw out
the poison
who, with her words,
re-define
your malaise?

Midnight Blues

Your words could drain an ocean
of its tears, you said,
I measure your madness
in months.
But what you never knew:
You crossed a room
and the moon followed,
you took a breath
and traffic stopped.

Forever ago.

And now the phone rings
at midnight
and it's no one (but it's you),
and you're not here
but here you are:

Somewhere down south,
getting wrecked at some bar,
thumbs circling an imaginary
globe and a glass
rimmed with salt, repeatedly.

Up here, I write poems and
answer phone calls at midnight
and the joke is still on me:

I write poems and
answer phones at midnight
and my words are changing
the levels of the sea.

Teeth

After a drink and a half
and feeling lonely
at midnight
it comes easy
to think of you.

To feel the weight of you
pushing down on me.
My legs wrapped tightly
around the hips
of some idea of us.

It's thumbs and lips
and teeth and tongue.
It's no on no.
It's nothing.

My gift to you

You wanted the moon
and here it is.

A fever dream
An eyelash wish.

(I would have given it
to you for nothing)

Can you feel me now?

Maybe
one day
these words will find you
and wrap themselves
around your heart,
the same way your fingers
used to curl around my throat.

Too tender
to take your breath away
but firm enough
to make you gasp.

Earthquake

Some heartbeats
are too loud in the night.
They make me think
of elephants
and earthquakes,
cracked asphalt
and shifting earth.
I shudder
but I listen.

The sound of morning
comes with its own
catastrophes,
so mesmerizing and severe—
that everything after
holds

disappointment

Guilt

Guilty hands
on spine
on hips.
It's come to this.
Lick your fingers.
Whet your lips.
Turn me over
like a page,
read me
like you would
a book.
I am words.
No more,
no less.
Now
taste your fingers
sweet with poison,
laced
with bitterness.

Madness

It's there at 3 AM,
mad and raging
like a fire two houses down.
The tuning up of 100 violins
downstairs,
when the ring slides off
and the panties drop.
Someone half-alive
and barely breathing
on some Californian beach.
A stillborn ripped away
from its mother's
grasping hands.
Loss replaced by loss.
Madness is silent.
Listen closely.
Try again.
You, too, will hear it scream.

Fracture

I carry something inside of me,
cracked and splintered and it always hurts.
It tortures me, but it's best this way,
it's better than feeling nothing at all.

I wish I didn't have to think about it
on nights like tonight,
when the loneliness curls itself
around me like a newborn child.

Perhaps this will forever be the ache,
the broken bone I did not want set,
I did not want healed.
So I could feel it at all times,
fractured, and hiding,
somewhere inside myself.

Tightrope

The steady things
that keep me
have shifted
in the night.
They are echoes
only silence can hold.

Push me
  off the cliff
pull me
  from this rope
I'm dancing on
I'm dangling from.

Your song plays
in my off-kilter heart
again
and again.

(The things you tell me at 5 AM.)

Chevron incision

I have been told
that late at night and here,
only you and I exist.

Mid-axillary and
halfway to the
chambers of the heart,
I carry you
in the hairline fractures
of marrow and ribs,
between the spaces
of muscle and sinew
and fingertips.

Show me the history
of your heart.
Teach me
the anatomy of love.

Moon

He was too far away
to ever truly be loved by me.

But like the moon
he was my light
and when the days grew dark

—he shined.

Liar

I cannot sleep.
My bones ache.
I bleed inside
with need.

His lips whisper
a silent prayer
above my chest,
but I've grown deaf.

His words betray.
My heart does not.
It knows who I love best.

Gone

I crave and dread
the silence

the tenderness
the violence

the slowest kiss
your hurried scrawl

bewilderment
the sudden fall

your hands and hips
and summer rain

you're here
and you are gone again.

Suicide

The girl downstairs
plays her
sad records all night,
they're scratched
and they skip
but she tries
again and again,
most nights until 3 AM.

I laugh and cry
and I have nowhere
to hide.
This is my life now:
Skipped records
and 3 AM suicide.

Intruder

4:30 pm
You'll soon be gone
and I—
left to myself again.
I feel the heaviness now,
sinking in,
and the sun draws yellow
cobwebs onto walls
that were not built
for our storms and
should-have-beens.

You, Stranger,
you are beautiful but you
should not be here.
What good is your heart?
and—
who let you in?

Not mine

2am
too late
and I am here
and he sleeps
elsewhere
and I
no longer
reach
for him,
his hands
in someone
else's now.

Captain and Coke

It's a brand-new thing
chasing back your name
with tears and a drink,
between years ago and now
and all the nights
of needing you
that fell in between.

Sip and spit
      just to feel
the burn again

Suck and swallow
      and I wonder when
or what it will take to
    un-
      yearn you again.

Aching silence

I long for these nights
to be over.
This aching silence
no longer
needing to be filled
with sounds of ruined love
and lies.

Anyone

Be the weight
that lays on my lungs,
the heaviness
that makes it hard
to breathe, effortlessly.

Carve yourself
into me, rob me of the
ability to remember
the touch of anyone
who is not you.

Forget this

Don't
so desperately try
to hold on to me.

For every beautiful woman
there is a man
who is tired of her
and that is me
and this is you.

Your love
was never worth
its weight
and most things
are not worth
their keep.

Let my hand drop,
let my name slip
from your mind.
It's ok.
That is me
and this is you.
And we all have someone
to lose.

ABOUT THE AUTHOR

Diana was born and raised in Germany and moved to the U.S. shortly before her 19th birthday. She now lives near the Florida beaches with a husband and 2 sons and spends her days writing.